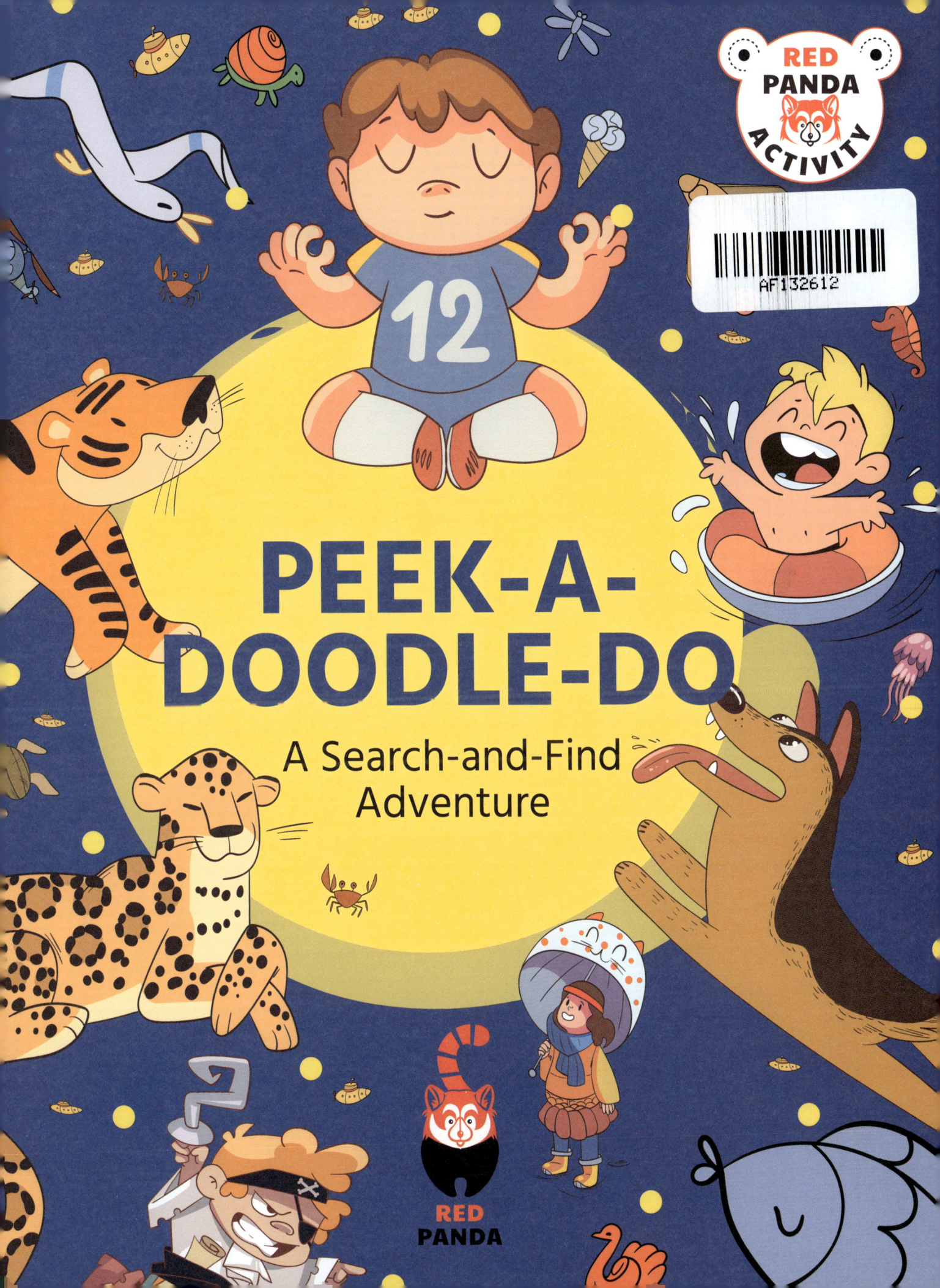

Published by Red Panda, an imprint of Westland Books, a division of Nasadiya Technologies Private Limited, in 2025

No. 269/2B, First Floor, 'Irai Arul', Vimalraj Street, Nethaji Nagar, Alapakkam Main Road, Maduravoyal, Chennai 600095

Westland, the Westland logo, Red Panda and the Red Panda logo are the trademarks of Nasadiya Technologies Private Limited, or its affiliates.

Copyright © Nasadiya Technologies Private Limited, 2025

ISBN: 9789371971126

10 9 8 7 6 5 4 3 2 1

All rights reserved

Book design by Mukul Chand

Images sourced from Shutterstock

Printed at Nutech Print Services Pvt. Ltd

No part of this book may be reproduced, or stored in a retrieval system, or transmitted in any form or by any means, electronic, mechanical, photocopying, recording, or otherwise, without express written permission of the publisher.

Find 10 objects hidden in the picture below.

Find a green bird.

Count the number of cats and dogs each.

1

Find 10 objects hidden in the picture below.

How many bottles can you spot?

Name all the fruits in the fridge.

Find 10 objects hidden in the picture below.

Can you count the dots on the girl's pillow?

Can you guess what time of the day it is?

3

Find 10 objects hidden in the picture below.

Count the number of paw prints on the sofa.

What kind of person do you think the dog's human is—a clean freak or not?

Find 12 objects hidden in the picture below.

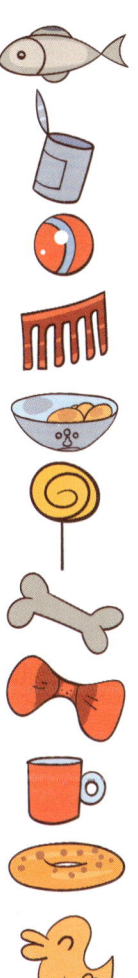

One of Jen's pets is napping under the umbrella. Can you find it?

Can you spot the creature that loves to leap and croak?

Find 8 objects hidden in the picture below.

How many fish are swimming to the left and how many to the right?

The cats are peeking into the aquarium! One fish looks really sad. Can you draw a circle around the fish that is having a bad day?

Find 20 objects hidden in the picture below.

How many hamsters can you find in the cage?

Find 15 objects hidden in the picture below.

Three of the runners have blue shoes. See if you can spot them.

Spot the runner with a three-digit number on their shirt.

Find 10 objects hidden in the picture below.

How many stripes can you count on the little girl's socks?

Everyone in the picture is wearing something with a geometrical pattern. Can you find the one person whose pattern looks different from the others?

Find 10 objects hidden in the picture below.

Circle the one guest who is the odd one among all the other animals.

Gigi's celebrating! Do you know how old he turned today?

Find 10 objects hidden in the picture below.

Look at the leaves. Can you guess what season it is?

What do hungry bunnies love to munch on?

Find 10 objects hidden in the picture below.

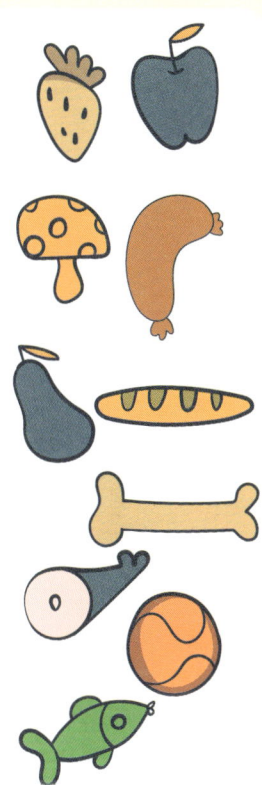

Look closely. What items can you find on the pantry shelves?

Can you find the ingredients needed to make *puris*?

Find 10 objects hidden in the picture below.

Can you spot the two animals that live on land and in water?

Cats and dogs are having a great time in the beach. What season do you think it is?

Find 8 objects hidden in the picture below.

How many shoes can you spot on this page?

If each friend brought two snacks and three books, how many snacks and books are there in total?

Find 10 objects hidden in the picture below.

How many cats can you find in the picture?

Are there more pets or people in this picture?

Find 8 objects hidden in the picture below.

FIND THE **WOLF** IN THE PICTURE

How many species of farm animals are there on the page?

Find 10 objects hidden in the picture below.

How many people are carrying treat bags.

Find 10 objects hidden in the picture below.

FIND THE **TIGER** IN THE PICTURE

How many animals are there in the picture?

Find 10 objects hidden in the picture below.

FIND **SKUNK** IN THE PICTURE

How many slices of watermelon can you spot?

Someone in the family loves music! Can you find the instrument they brought to the picnic?

Find 10 objects hidden in the picture below.

FIND CAT IN THE PICTURE

Count the number of ornaments on the Christmas tree.

Find 10 animals hidden in the picture below.

Count the number of hens in the picture.

Find 11 objects hidden in the picture below.

FIND THE **RABBIT** IN THE PICTURE

Add up all the dots on the two dices. What's the total?

How many playing cards are floating around the magician?

Find 10 objects hidden in the picture below.

FIND **OWL** IN THE PICTURE

How many readers can you spot in this picture?

Find 10 objects hidden in the picture below.

Max is deep in the jungle on a special mission: he needs to find the magnificent Big Cats! Can you help him by pointing them out?

25

Find 10 objects hidden in the picture below.

Which animal is called the king of the jungle? Can you spot him here?

Find 10 objects hidden in the picture below.

How many umbrellas are there in the picture?

Find 10 objects hidden in the picture below.

TRUE or FALSE?
There are three cats in the picture.

Find 10 animals hidden in the picture below.

FIND THE TURTLE IN THE PICTURE

ANIMALS OF THE AFRICAN SAVANNAH
ELEPHANTS • WILDEBEEST • GIRAFFES • LIONS • PARROTS • MONKEY • HIPPOS • RHINOCEROS • OSTRICHES • ZEBRAS

Spot a baby lion. Do you know what is it called?

29

Find 10 objects hidden in the picture below.

How many aquatic animals can you spot in the image?

Crabs have feet. Octopus have tentacles and fish have ___ .

Find 10 objects hidden in the picture below.

Can you count how many roses are blooming in the picture?

Can you spot the rose that's still a little bud?

Find mistakes in the picture below.

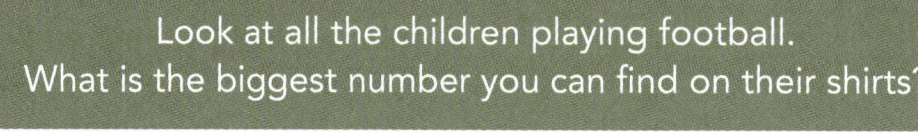

Look at all the children playing football.
What is the biggest number you can find on their shirts?

FIND 12 RABBITS IN PICTURE

How many sports are being played in the picture?

Find 10 objects hidden in the picture below.

Can you count the number of wheels in the picture?

The Zoom family have packed too much stuff for their camping trip. One of them look really scared. Look carefully and circle their face.

34

Find 10 objects hidden in the picture below.

Which tree has the least coconuts?

Sasha is having a relaxing beach day. How many seashells can you spot scattered in the sand around her towel?

Find 10 objects hidden in the picture below.

Count the unicorns with wings and those without.

How many unicorns are wearing their hearts on their sleeves (and skin)?

Find 8 objects hidden in the picture below.

Do you know our national bird? Can you find it here?

Can you name each of these animals and birds?

37

Find hidden objects in the picture below.

Look closely: there are frogs everywhere! Can you count them all?

What are the cats waiting for so eagerly? Look at the picture for clues!

Answers

Page 1

6 dogs and 16 cats

Page 2

Apples and grapes; 5 bottles

Page 3

20 dots on the pillow; It's 6.15 a.m.

Page 4

7 paw prints; The dog's human is very messy.

Page 5

Page 6

7 to the left and 9 to the right;

Page 7

7 hamsters

Page 8-9

Page 10

8 stripes on the socks

Page 11

3-years-old

Page 12

It's Autumn/ Fall; Bunnies love to munch on carrots.

Page 13

1 cat and 3 mice; Salt and flour are used to make *puris*.

Page 14

Crab; It's summer.

Page 15

2 shoes; 6 snacks and 9 books

Page 16

3 cats; More humans (5) than pets (2)

Page 17

2 farm animals—sheep and hen

Page 18

3 treat bags

Page 19

Dogs, tiger, lion, hippo, hen, rabbit, pig, tortoise, cat, birds, zebra

Page 20

Three slices of watermelon; Guitar

Page 21

23 ornaments

Page 22

12 hens

Page 23

15 flying cards; 11

Page 24

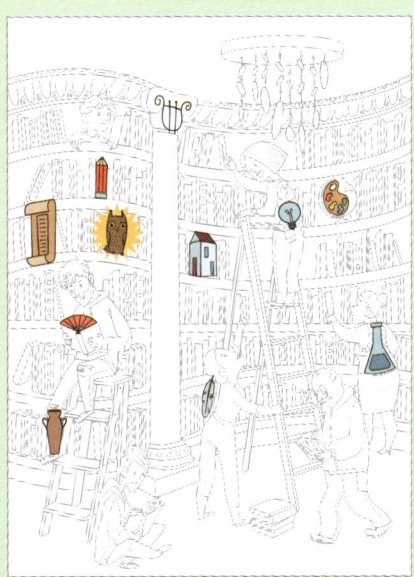

6 readers and one spectator

Page 25

Page 26

Page 27

7 umbrellas

Page 28

Page 29

Page 30

False.

A baby lion is called a cub.

Fish have fins.

Page 31

Page 32-33

12; Football, Ice skating; Yoga, Boxing, Swimming, Long jump, Skiing

Page 34

8 wheels

Page 35

10 seashells

Page 36

1 with a bow.

Page 37

Peachock, Zebra, Yak, Goat, Flamengo, Ostrich, Reindeer, Camel, Gorilla, Emu; Hidden - Lion, Hippo, Giraffe, Crocodile, Elephant, Tiger, Rhino, Penguin

Page 38-39

11 frogs; The cats are waiting for fish